SUICIDE SLOWLY

SCOTT SHAW

BUDDHA ROSE PUBLICATIONS

First Edition 1989
Second Edition 2011

ISBN 10: 1-877792-14-4
ISBN 13: 978-1-877792-14-4

10 9 8 7 6 5 4 3 2 1
Printed in the United States of America

2

SUICIDE SLOWLY

"what are you up to?"

"suicide slowly."

    for all of those
    who hold onto the dream
    or wish for
    the ultimate kiss of death

    for everything
        that is worth having
    but the first step in getting it
        is just too hard to take
    for all the tears
        that are cried
    to no one else's ears

    and when tomorrow's
    promises
    mean nothing more than
    today's lies

    just kiss me goodbye

    I choose suicide slowly

awh...

you're not even an artist
if you haven't spent
four or five christmas' alone
have a few line on your face
cried yourself to sleep
more than a few times
and walked down too many streets
      alone

alone, while others
      walked hand-in-hand

and if you think artists
have women
no way
you're not even close
until you have spent
more nights alone
than sleeping
bound and embraced
engulfed and intertwined

an artist
you don't want to be that

a girl
she is waiting for me
waiting
on the other side of town
waiting and wanting
desiring and needing
over there
on the other side of town

and yes,
we are world's apart

    to know me
    is to love
    so I have heard it said
    said and spoken
    to know her
    is to love her
    but loving her
    it is the death of me

sanctuary in a glass/suicide in a
cup

and her love
it runs through my veins

like a drug
a piercing poison/fierce addition
stringing my soul along

    and with nowhere left to run
    no one left to run to
    I cross the city/I cross the
    town
    I fall into her arms
    and for a moment
    my addiction
    is met/fulfilled

    to know her
    is to love her
    to know her
    is killing me

        sublime obsession
        in a broken world
        so supreme

    I love her
    I do not want to love her

4

sitting in the fading sun
a cup of *java* in my hand
a brief hollow/hallowed wind
blows
as I stare into my own disparity
looking down the throat
of my own confusion
my inability to conform

and yes,
I have a million things to do
a million and one
if you please
and money,
well no,
I don't have any
they, the world
tells me that I should get a job

thank you but no thank you
someone has to die
still dreaming

and yes, I still hold onto
the dream

as I wait in this afternoon
for a miracle to come down

     die to dream
         dream to die

waiting w/ a cup of the *java*
in my hand

     as a hollow/hallowed wind
       gently blows

scream
and there is no one there to hear it
is it a scream at all?

die
it touched a fantasy deep inside
but it was gone

live
when/where/why/how

drink
I think so
it is easier that way

6

the sun in my eyes
the wind cools its blow
the sound of the city
pounds in my head
I look
and there is no place
left to run

     the nighttime it is for
     whispers

     the daytime it is for
     screams

     and the lost
     are left intermixed
     with the living
     pretending to be
     but not being the same

the red wine flows like blood
the blood
that poured out of her veins

    I was not there to see it
    given the chance
    I would have
    walked the other way

drink me into drunken stupor
her passion was my promise
a promise
I never could have kept

drink me down
like this glass I finish
finish too fast
the fact to finish
my taste buds
they have become so numb

    I could have loved her
    didn't really want to

didn't really know how
I told her I did anyway

words,
they just don't mean a thing
not anything at all

a bottle finished
another bottle down
a life gone
wrists wide open

corkscrew
wine
red

another bottle in my hand
not like life
not like women
not like
one chance
is all you ever get

slap me with your promiscuity
tell me that you just don't care
hit me with all of your
passionate dispassion
me too, me too

give me a whore/hand me a slut
gutter tramps like I
who walks the night

that is where life is lived
where the truth is known

> leave india for the holy
> israel for the fool
> I'll take southeast asia
> where it just doesn't matter
>   anymore

> I'm tired of chasing
> that vestal virgin
> dream

9

sitting staring out of
bamboo shades
bamboo shades
lead to the/a summers' day

    bamboo shades/prison bars
      life in the big city

watching a movie on T.V.
isolation
a glass of wine, red
isolation

    the unit of isolation
    easy unity
    passive submission
    a saved life
    in an elementary vision
    bound from the world
    saved from the dis-ease

    but desire it still hides
    in every corner

and personally
I prefer the chance

moments
    in the life of an
unwilling recluse

sip the grape
it has become
so un-fashionable/so uncool
sip the grape
while american society
the mindless masses
follow all the trends
listen to all the lies

sip the grape
drink down a moment of illusion
in a life that passes by
all too fast

night time
       all the time

sometimes I would just
       prefer to
       go to bed

women or alone
always running
a need to run
somewhere/nowhere
like jogging on a tread mill
like tires in the sand
like ice in the sunshine
or a greased female body
       next to mine

to bed
but three is poetry to write
literature to create
and you know
that I am years behind
all the going to nowhere
the cuming, not the becoming

20

nighttime, all the time

and the chase after
that oh so allusive
reason for the literature
reason for the poetry
female form
of a feminine dream

a park
surrounded by a city
I listen to the hum
it can be heard from all around
from all directions
shattering
the almost silence
breaking it w/ an almost sound

someone's hard earned day
ticks on/ticks by
I spend it
like the dollars and cents
of the moving world
conquering all
accomplishing nothing

me, I would prefer to listen
to the almost silence
to the constant sound
feel the perfection
of the imperfection
of life that ticks on and on

13

I am surround by time
ticking by
    and you know
    that there isn't
    a thing I can do about it

    I went out on my patio
        this evening

   a patio
      that overlooks the sea

   I watched the sunset
      but it was gone
      before it could be
      grasped

and I guess
that it would not be so bad
but I feel like
I have so much bullshit
so much other bullshit
that I should be doing
that is, other than

spending credit card money
that I don't have

making love to a chick
that I don't dig
and running somewhere
              to nowhere
        across the off reaches
              of the globe

but then what is art
I guess it is feeling good
doing what you are doing
but what about
when you are an artist
feeling bad
about what you are not doing

        so tick-tock
              fuck the clock

14

a dream just too tired to be lived
too tired to be known

with the
pounding/hyperventilating
heart attack
of the known world
pounding down
on my soul
there is so little room
left for vision

so jump start
the life start
back to where it all began

    fall down
    one too many times
    there is no one to give
    the dreamer a hand
        left to their own devise
        of the self demise

a drink = a dream
a kiss = a moment
but nothing always = nothing

15

hospital walls
    gray,
    white,
    light green,
    faded blue

into her room
she lay on the bed
it almost looks high tech
almost fashion-passion
like the style which she embraced

chrome metal
risen steel boundaries
holding her in
like the bars of a prison
the sweet bird in a cage

and plastic tubes
they form the veins
which led into her arm

as her skin
blended into the aloneness
of the white hospital sheets

who else has known them
who else has been trapped
by their grasp

    yes, you are dying
    please go to a better place
        a place
    where you will be happy

    go to somewhere
    where the living
    does not make you sad

    and you will live in my heart
        forever
    forever and ever and ever
    until someday
    when I join you

    where life is not so hard
    and the dreams
    they do not crumble

like so many crumbs
in our hands

I love you, good bye

lay on the couch
all day long
damned, if I know where to run

t.v. on
pre-wash the brain-wash
    why?
does your brain need washing?

    glass of wine
    in my hand
    a bottle or three
    over there

    a babe
    or two
    across the city
        they are just not worth
    the drive

so $0 = 0$
nothing all the same
let me lay here
doing the nothing

nothing
the purest form of art

a world that is going someplace
a world that is going by
a million millionaires
a billion wanta be/will be/could be
talking of their finances
speaking of the cars they drive

me
I prefer to refer
to dreaming visions

me
I would rather not live
than to live the lie

love poetry on a napkin
and the days that do not mean
   anything at all

   the L.A. sun is pouncing
   pounding hard
   on the plexiglas patio
   on which I sit

   people eat
      all around me

   discussion life
      politics
      boxing
      and karma

   as the stylish cars
   motor down
      wilshire boulevard
        they cruise
        right on by me

and me
I sit here
discussing the silence
living the dream
for whatever it is worth

and I write of a love
that I ran away from today
yes, it was just this morning
after we made love last night
4:32 AM
I know
because I looked at the clock

but rich babes now poor
all they want to do
is complain
insult the dreams
of a dreamer
remind you
of all that you are not

but all is nothing anyway
and you can see
how fast it goes away
rich babes now poor

their eyes
promise a life of disaster

I walked out
with an ounce of pride
which sure beats
living through
a hell of dispassion

and so
here I sit
awaiting breakfast
11:28 A.M.
bombay burger
as the sun
pours onto the plexiglas
creating kill humidity
reminding me of bombay

making me feel/making me wish
                that I was back there
                in india again

java/the grape
stay awake/alter the state
poetry to write
paintings to bring into existence

like new souls being born
rhythms being composed
a reason/a purpose
late night/all night
leave the days
 for the working
 the saints of this world
 the night
 it is for the dreamers

 a drink from a cup
 a sip from a glass
 like poison/like passion
 like passages
 a key to this night

slice me another cup of the java
stay up all night long

a glass of the grape
to take the edge off
while I live the dream

here
where nothing really matters
where I melt
     into the aloneness of art

exist
in the nothing worth living for
and dream
     oh yes
     I do have a few dreams

3:00 A.M.
and another drink
for another reason
   god
   I am going to be sick
   tomorrow

throw a frozen pizza
into the oven
and it just doesn't mean
anything at all

like the drink
like the money
like the babe
I made love to tonight

there she is
over there
passed out in my bed

the nothing of conquest
the lust of momentary love

a moment lived
only for the poetry

the price
it is always paid later

20

and the night
it goes down hard
but its better
than sitting at home
being married/getting old

> w/ every dance
>> there is another chance

so morning
well, afternoon is here
out of bed
time to lick my wounds
move from the bed
to the couch
my dick
still a bit twisted
too much sex
too much cocaine
evening last

my stomach
none too pretty
a bit too much of the drink

but a moment to dream
a life to steal
and it all mean nothing
anyway

fuck the holy
they know nothing
leave the living
for the dreamers
who have experienced
it all

I am strutting my bad self
in this khaki style clothing store
when up comes this babe
rap'n to her friend
in the *nehongo*
(japanese)

yeah, she was fine
move on/move in
strut in/strut out

finally
she and her child bearing/child
     carrying friend
were separate
     apart
     I move on over
     give her a sweet little word
     a speech/a saying
     in her native tongue

we spoke of tokyo
we spoke of L.A.

age and names

and then
      up comes here friend
      if looks could kill...

so back up/back off
went and paid for the clothing
w/ plastic passion
      money
      that I do not have

she came up to pay after me
I said,
"see you later.
      someplace/some dream,"
I spoke to her in japanese

I walked out the door
in all my empty
      alone glory
      and style

      another one of those dreams
      that just begged to happen
      another one of those times
      when I should have

done this
could have done that

a moment of life
cast,
only to this poetry
and the *never-never-land*
of what might have been

the night hits hard
lost in the confusion
of this lost life
I drive down the boulevard
me, in my 1964 porsche

I could stop/I should go home
but fuck it
I drive on
into the abyss of nowhere
      supremely fast

the world cries out to me
to pay my bills
the passion screams to me
to spend money I do not have

my bad little '64 of a 356 sc
it was suggested
that I sell it
sell it, to pay the rent

      now, I guess I am a few
      years older than it

six
if I count them on the dial

and no-one/no-thing
last forever

so, I look
I look, to the
        rear view mirror
look at my face
look into my own eyes
but sell it/sell me
no thank you
I think it is time
for both of us
to roll up shop
and die

drive some-where/no-where
like, you know
        driving along
        and put the
        pedal to the metal
        punch it real hard
        feel the g-force
        pull me back

and guideme/guide us
into *never-never-land*

where the rent is free
no break downs

no bills to pay
and it's gotta
feel better

a whole lot better than this

About the Author:

Scott Shaw is a prolific poet, author, actor, composer, photographer, and filmmaker. Shaw was born and spent his formative years in Hollywood, California and has since spent years of his life living in various geographical locations throughout Asia. His poetry and literary fiction were first published in literary journals in the late 1970s. He continued forward to have several works of poetry and literature published in book form during the 1980s. As the 1990s dawned, Shaw's writings began to be embraced in Spiritual and Martial Art circles. From this, he has authored a number of books on Zen Buddhism, Yoga, and the Martial Arts, published by large publishing houses.

Scott Shaw's
Books-In-Print include:

The Little Book of Yoga Breathing
Nirvana in a Nutshell
About Peace:
    108 Ways to Be at Peace When
    Things Are Out of Control
Zen O'clock: Time To Be
The Tao of Self Defense
Samurai Zen
The Ki Process: Korean Secrets
    for Cultivating Dynamic
    Energy
The Warrior is Silent:
    Martial Arts
    and the Spiritual Path
Hapkido:
    The Korean Art of
    Self Defense
Hapkido: Essays on Self-Defense
Taekwondo Basics
Advanced Taekwondo
Chi Kung For Beginners
Mastering Health:
    The A to Z of Chi Kung

Cambodia Refugees
       in Long Beach, California
China Deep
Essence: The Zen of Everything
Shanghai Whispers
       Shanghai Screams
Shattered Thoughts
Junk: The Back Streets of Bangkok
The Passionate Kiss of Illusion
TKO: Lost Nights in Tokyo
Bangkok and the Nights
       of Drunken Stupor
No Kisses for the Sinner
Zen Buddhism:
       The Pathway to Nirvana
Zen: Tales from the Journey
Zen in the Blink of an Eye
Yoga: A Spiritual Guidebook
Marguerite Duras
       and Charles Bukowski:
The Yin and Yang of Modern
Erotic Literature

www.ingramcontent.com/pod-product-compliance
Lightning Source LLC
Chambersburg PA
CBHW060810110426
42739CB00032BA/3164

* 9 7 8 1 8 7 7 7 9 2 1 4 4 *